BOOKWORMS

Riding to the Rescue!

# Coast Guard Boats

B.J. Best

Cavendish Square
New York

Published in 2018 by Cavendish Square Publishing, LLC
243 5th Avenue, Suite 136, New York, NY 10016



First Edition



Website: cavendishsq.com



CPSIA Compliance Information: Batch #CS17CSQ

All websites were available and accurate when this book was sent to press.

Library of Congress Cataloging-in-Publication Data

Names: Best, B. J., 1976- author.
Title: Coast Guard boats / B.J. Best.
Description: New York : Cavendish Square Publishing, [2018] | Series: Riding to the rescue! | Includes index.
Identifiers: LCCN 2016050016 (print) | LCCN 2016050266 (ebook) | ISBN 9781502625762 (pbk.) | ISBN 9781502625564 (6 pack) | ISBN 9781502625687 (library bound) | ISBN 9781502625625 (E-book)
Subjects: LCSH: United States. Coast Guard--Juvenile literature. | Government vessels--United States--Juvenile literature.
Classification: LCC VG53 .B47 2017 (print) | LCC VG53 (ebook) | DDC 363.28/60284--dc23
LC record available at https://lccn.loc.gov/2016050016

The photographs in this book are used by permission and through the courtesy of:
Cover U.S. Coast Guard/Science Faction/Getty Images Entertainment/Getty Images; p. 5 Mark Conlin/Alamy Stock Photo; p. 7 Craig Tuttle/Perspectives/Getty Images Entertainment/Getty Images; p. 9 Glenn Koenig/Contributor/Los Angeles Times/Getty Images Entertainment/Getty Images; p. 11 Federico Rostagno/Shutterstock.com; p. 13 Justin Sullivan/Staff/Getty Images News/Getty Images Entertainment/Getty Images; p. 15 David Lau/dvidshub.net/Wikimedia Commons; p. 17 Gabe Souza/Contributor/Portland Press Herald/Getty Images Entertainment/Getty Images; p. 19 Scott Olson/Staff/Getty Images News/Getty Images Entertainment/Getty Images, p. 21 Marc Hoberman/Corbis Documentary/Getty Images Entertainment/Getty Images.

Printed in the United States of America

# Contents

A fishing boat has stopped working!

It needs help.

It calls the **Coast** Guard!

Z6427
JULIE KRISTINE

The Coast Guard works
in lakes.

It works in rivers.

It works off of the coast.

The coast is where the sea
meets the land.

U. S. COAST GUARD
563

The Coast Guard uses many boats.

A **utility** boat can do many jobs.

It can rescue people.

41373

Some boats work with **buoys**.

Buoys show other boats where to go.

The Coast Guard keeps **ports** safe.

It makes sure laws are followed.

It stops bad people from getting in.

25151
U.S. COAST GUARD

The Coast Guard uses big boats on the ocean.

A **cutter** is longer than 65 feet (20 meters).

People can live on cutters.

U.S. COAST GUARD
87314

Some Coast Guard boats do special things.

An icebreaker smashes ice.

Then other boats can travel through icy water.

65609

An airboat has a fan on the back.

It can go places other boats can't.

It can go in swamps. It can go down flooded streets.

PANTHER

The Coast Guard helps people on the water.

It keeps us safe!

U.S. COAST GUARD
33125

# New Words

**buoys** (BOO-ees) Floating things that tell boats where to go.

**coast** (COHST) The place where the ocean and land touch.

**cutter** (CUT-ter) A large boat.

**ports** (PORTS) Places on shore where boats can stop.

**utility** (yu-TIH-leh-tee) Able to do many different things.

# Index

# About the Author

**B.J. Best** lives in Wisconsin with his wife and son. He has written many other books for children. He has never been lost at sea.

## About BOOKWORMS

Bookworms help independent readers gain reading confidence through high-frequency words, simple sentences, and strong picture/text support. Each book explores a concept that helps children relate what they read to the world they live in.